Little Dinosaur ABC Coloring Book

Little
DINOSAUR ABC
Coloring Book

Winky Adam

DOVER PUBLICATIONS, INC.
Mineola, New York

Bibliographical Note

Little Dinosaur ABC Coloring Book is a new work, first
published by Dover Publications, Inc., in 1998.

International Standard Book Number

ISBN-13: 978-0-486-40301-4
ISBN-10: 0-486-40301-7

Manufactured in the United States by Courier Corporation
40301711   2014
www.doverpublications.com

Note

Young paleontologists will love learning the alphabet with the help of the twenty-six little dinosaur friends in this book. As kids color each letter of the alphabet, they can also enjoy coloring the dinosaur whose name begins with the corresponding letter. There are lots of fun facts to read and a pronunciation guide makes it easy to say the dinosaurs' names.

Little Dinosaur ABC Coloring Book

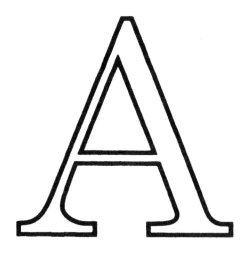

Apatosaurus (ah-PAT-uh-SAWR-us), also called Brontosaurus, liked to eat fish and plants from the sea.

Apatosaurus

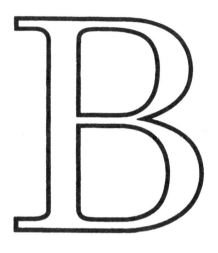

Brachiosaurus (BRAK-ee-uh-SAWR-us) was one of the largest dinosaurs that ever lived.

Brachiosaurus

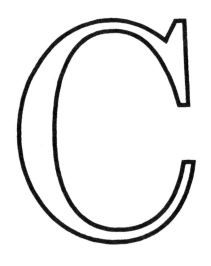

Compsognathus (comp-sog-NAY-thus) was the tiniest of all meat-eating dinosaurs.

Compsognathus

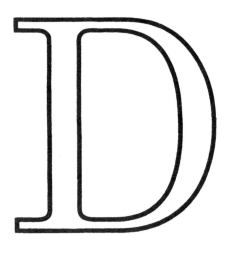

Deinonychus (dy-no-NIKE-us) was a small and fierce hunter.

Deinonychus

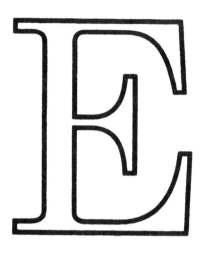

Elasmosaurus (e-LAZ-muh-SAWR-us)
used its long neck to catch fish.

Elasmosaurus

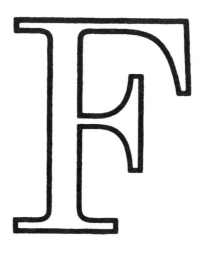

Fabrosaurus (FAB-ruh-SAWR-us) had
to run very fast to avoid being eaten
by bigger dinosaurs.

Fabrosaurus

Geosaurus (GEE-uh-SAWR-us), a swimming dinosaur, looked like a crocodile with seal flippers.

Geosaurus

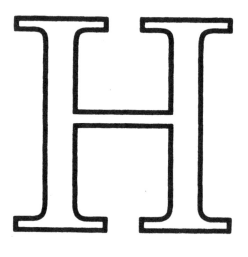

Bones of the Hadrosaurus (HAD-ruh-SAWR-us) were the first dinosaur bones discovered in America.

Hadrosaurus

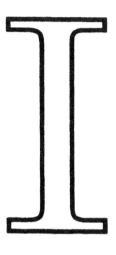

Iguanodon (ih-GWAHN-uh-DON) was
a very large plant eater.

Iguanodon

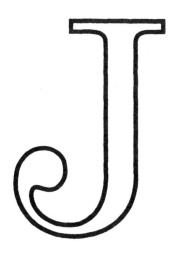

Janenschia (YAN-ENSH-ee-a) could raise its neck to eat from the trees.

Janenschia

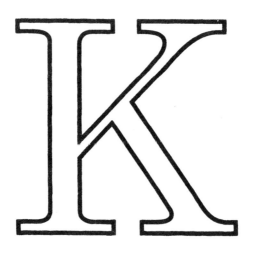

Kentrosaurus (KEN-truh-SAWR-us),
like its larger cousin Stegosaurus,
had sharp, pointed spikes on its back.

Kentrosaurus

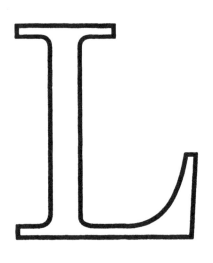

Lambeosaurus (LAM-bee-oh-SAWR-us) had a narrow beak and a crest on its head.

Lambeosaurus

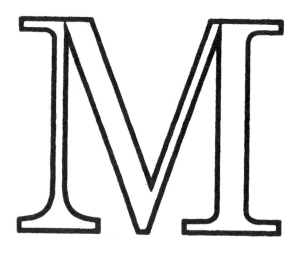

The bones of Megalosaurus (MEG-ah-loh-SAWR-us), or great lizard, were first discovered in England more than 150 years ago.

Megalosaurus

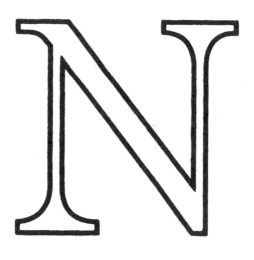

Nanotyrannus (NAN-oh-tie-RAN us) walked on two feet and lived in what is now Montana.

Nanotyrannus

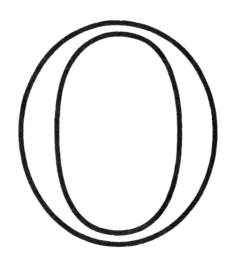

Oviraptor (Ove-ih-RAP-tor) had no teeth.

Oviraptor

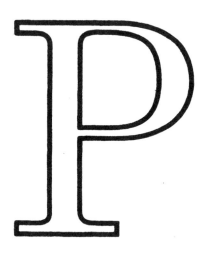

Parasaurolophus (par-a-sawr-oh-LOAF-us) had a large crest at the back of its head.

Parasaurolophus

Quetzalcoatlus (ket-SOL-kuh-WAT-lus) flew above land looking for dead dinosaurs to eat.

Quetzalcoatlus

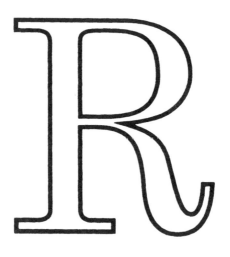

Rhamphorhynchus (ram-for-INK-us),
a flying reptile, probably speared fish
with its sharp teeth.

Rhamphorhynchus

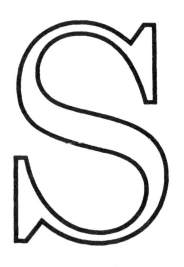

Stegosaurus (steg-uh-SAWR-us), who was as big as a house, had a brain as small as a walnut.

Stegosaurus

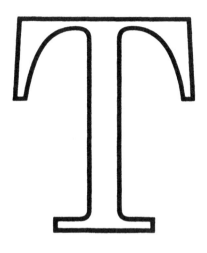

Tyrannosaurus (tye-RAN-uh-SAWR-us) was the largest meat-eating animal who ever lived.

Tyrannosaurus

Ultrasaurus (UL-truh-SAWR-us), or "ultra lizard," walked on four feet and ate plants.

Ultrasaurus

Velociraptor (veh-LOSS-i-RAP-tor)
was a fierce, meat-eating dinosaur
about the size of an average person.

Velociraptor

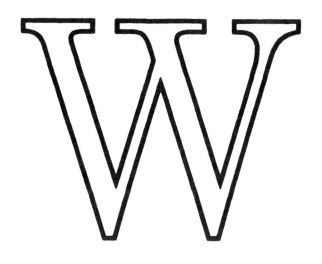

Wannanosaurus (wan-an-oh SAWR-us), a very small dinosaur, lived in what is now China.

Wannanosaurus

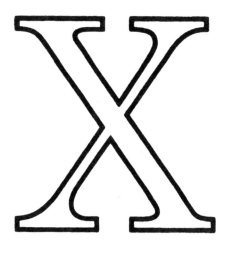

Xenotarsosaurus (zen-oh-tar-soh-SAWR-us), or "strange ankle lizard," was a large meat-eater from the region that is now Argentina.

Xenotarsosaurus

57

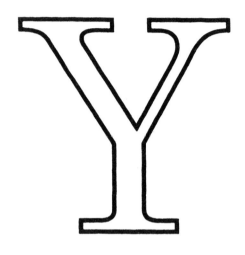

Yandusaurus (YAN-doo-SAWR-us)
walked on two feet and ate plants.

Yandusaurus

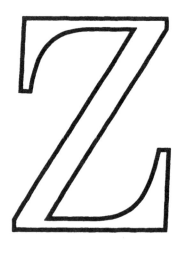

Zephyrosaurus (ZEF-ero-SAWR-us), a small plant-eater, had very sharp teeth.

Zephyrosaurus

Use these pages to draw your own dinosaurs